Memories LAST FOREVER

journal belongs to...

© 2016 Ranch House Press
All rights reserved. Printed in the United States of America.

www.annettebridges.com

ISBN: 978-1-946371-08-9

Journal Prompts

Memories Last Forever

Write, doodle, paint or scapbook about your memories this month!

1. One place you go when you need a change of scenery.
2. Can you remember your mom's or grandmother's kitchen? Use sight or smell words to describe it.
3. Write about a holiday memory. Where did you go? What did you do? What foods do you remember?
4. Describe your favorite hideaway.
5. Do you have quirky or interesting relatives on your family tree? Describe one or two of them.
6. What is your earliest memory?
7. How have childhood favorites impacted you? (toys, cartoons, books, etc)
8. What event in your childhood had the most impact on your life as an adult?
9. What moment in your life have you felt most loved?
10. What was the greatest challenge of your life so far?
11. The most surprised I've ever been...
12. The most fun I've ever had...
13. One story you love to tell.
14. A song that you've danced to.
15. A song that calms you down.
16. Make a list of at least 5 memories that you would describe as the best feeling in the world.
17. Make a list of 10 memories you're most thankful for.
18. Write a poem about a memory that you have when you come across a specific smell or image.
19. Recall an important time in your life when you made a fresh start or tried something new for the very first time.
20. Think of a time you traveled somewhere completely new. Try to recall how you felt as you absorbed the unknown.
21. Find a favorite photograph from your past. What is it about this photograph that makes it stand out as a favorite? What emotions stir up?
22. Are you recording the stories of the photos you have taken? Are you noting the details that will trigger rich memories later on? It's never too late to begin. Start printing and adding photos and write one line for each photo to prompt your memory of what was happening or being felt and any other sensory details in your photographs.
23. Create a timeline of significant memories, milestones and moments of your life so far.
24. Who is someone you've lost? What are some of your memories about that person?
25. What are some of the memories you associate with springtime? With summer, fall, winter?
26. Write about some of your firsts? Day of school or college? Date? Car? House? Pet? Job?
27. What makes a friend unforgettable?
28. Do you have a ghost memory that haunts you? Something you wish you could forget?
29. What is the best advice you've ever been given?
30. Write a letter to your memories.

color your world

ABOUT the CREATOR

Annette Bridges is an author, publisher and women's retreat host on a mission to help every woman realize her story is extraordinary, valuable and noteworthy.

She has published the *Color Your World Journal Series* and formed a journal club to provide community, support and tools for women to record their ideas, feelings, experiences, memories and all the important details of their lives.

Before writing books and publishing journals and coloring books, this former public school and homeschool educator spent a decade writing hundreds of helpful, instructive, and light-hearted columns published by Texas newspapers, parenting magazines, websites and bloggers.

Annette lives on a Texas cattle ranch with her husband John, dachshund Lady and lots of cows. She can drive a tractor but only if wearing a fresh coat of lipstick and it's not her pedicure day!

You can learn more about Annette's books and products, blogs and videos as well as her women's retreats and other events at www.annettebridges.com.

Look for her on social media, too!

MESSAGE from the PUBLISHER

The **Color Your World Journal Series** is a pathway to self-discovery. It's where you write notes to yourself. Be your own cheerleader. Give yourself encouragement. Tell yourself what you're grateful for. Celebrate you!

There are countless reasons to keep a journal including collecting favorite recipes, listing goals and celebrating every experience and every one that's near and dear to you. A journal provides a home for the memories and lessons learned that you never want to forget.

Why a niche journal?

If you're anything like me, you have a journal (or even two or three journals) where you write anything and everything about anything and everything. My challenge comes when trying to find something I've written. I flip and flip through the pages of my two, three or four journals trying to find whatever it is. I never remember which journal I wrote down my whatever's!!

The solution? A niche journal! A journal that has a specific focus and theme! A journal where you can record your ideas, inspirations and things you want to remember in the appropriate journal.

Why big unlined paper?

Because big unlined paper is needed to record big ideas, dreams and memories! You need room to grow, stretch and expand. You need space to think beyond the confines of what you've always done, to pursue new dreams, discover your power and reimagine your purpose again and again. You need pages without lines and limitations to reconnect with your creative, perfectly imperfect self.

Plus, big unlined paper gives you space for more than words. You have plenty of room to doodle, draw or post photographs and clippings, too.

Why color is important?

When you journal, use colored pens and markers! Your world doesn't happen in black and white. Your life should be lived and written about in many colors. Even dark and sad memories feel lighter and brighter when told in color.

Journaling in color affects your mood and perception of your world. Colors evoke calm, cheer and comfort. Using color can lift your spirit and inspire your imagination. You may be surprised by all the beautiful benefits from adding more color into your life story.

When journaling, give yourself time to listen to your heart and reflect. Breathe in the moments. Feel. Be quiet. Let yourself be totally and thoroughly present with your thoughts. Let your heart transform you and teach you new insights. Open your mind to consider new ideas and possibilities. You may find that what your heart teaches will be life changing.

www.ingramcontent.com/pod-product-compliance
Lightning Source LLC
Chambersburg PA
CBHW051253110526

44588CB00025B/2973